T0161371

THE EIGHTH MOUNTAIN
POETRY PRIZE

THE EIGHTH MOUNTAIN POETRY PRIZE was established in 1988 in honor of the poets whose words envision and sustain the feminist movement, and in recognition of the major role played by women poets in creating the literature of their time. Women poets world-wide are invited to participate. One manuscript is selected each year by a poet of national reputation. Publication and an advance of one thousand dollars are funded by a private donor. *Fear of Subways* was selected by Marilyn Hacker to be the second winner of the Eighth Mountain Poetry Prize.

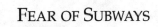

FEAR *of* SUBWAYS

Maureen Seaton

THE EIGHTH MOUNTAIN PRESS

PORTLAND · OREGON · 1991

First American Edition, 1991
2   3   4   5   6   7   8   9
Printed in the United States

Cover art is "Calling Forth Light" by Louise Williams,
reproduced by permission of the artist

Cover design by Marcia Barrentine
Book design by Ruth Gundle

Library of Congress Cataloging-in-Publication Data
Seaton, Maureen, 1947-
    Fear of subways / Maureen Seaton.—1st American ed.
      p. cm.
    ISBN 0-933377-16-9 (cloth)
    ISBN 0-933377-15-0 (paper)
    I. Title.
PS3569.E218F44   1991
811'.54—dc20   90-20220

THE EIGHTH MOUNTAIN PRESS
624 Southeast Twenty-ninth Avenue
Portland, Oregon 97214

Acknowledgements

"My Daughter Calls from a Halfway House in Houston" and "Photographing Horses" were published in *Chelsea*; "Mercedes Contemplates a Dive off Macmillan Wharf," "The Sacrifice," and "Truce" were published in *Colorado Review*; "The 8:48" was published in *Conditions*; "Citicard," "The Green Girl," and "The New Frontier" were published in *Downtown*; "Miracles" was published in *Iowa Review*; "Wintersong" was published in *Mankato Poetry Review*; "Christmas in the Midwest" and "Grief" were originally published and "Harlem" was reprinted in *Women in Exile* (Milkweed Editions, 1990); "Blood" was published in *New American Writing*; "The White Balloon" was originally published in *Outlook*; "Sonnets for a Single Mother" was published in *Ploughshares*; "Robin's Egg Blue" was published in *Poetry East*; "The White Balloon" was reprinted in *Poets for Life; Seventy-six Poets Respond to AIDS* (Crown Books, 1989); "Harlem" and "Mantras of the Homeless" were originally published in *River Styx*; "Preposition" was published in *Sonora Review*; "Stations" was published in *Southern Poetry Review*; "Glory Days" and "Witness" were published in *West Branch*.

I would like to express my gratitude to Glenn Sherratt and the Horace Mann School for their generous sharing of the Dorr Nature Laboratory in Washington, Connecticut, where some of these poems were conceived.

To Denise Duhamel, John Mason, Marialice Seaton, and Janet Zurheide, for love without conditions.

To Jennifer and Emily, for providing reasons.

To H.P.

for Lori

CONTENTS

HOW TO PRAY WITH A DYING WOMAN

ALCHEMY OF THE BODY

THE BED

Miracles

I am a miracle. Not
the only miracle. A fox

living in the dark perfume
of the reservoir

counts. You,
from your father's bed—

pure, intact, that
aqua light. Is it

greedy to gather berries
from the cliff-face,

gulp them, your other hand
free to clasp air? I

sensed a hollow where
his small flame lingered

among ash. Now color
pours from my hands.

When I touch you,
the heat startles. You say:

Here are the miracles:
the fox, the berries,

the child, grown lovely
and gorged with light.

Fear of Subways

Sonnets for a Single Mother

1. Fear of Subways

Sometimes in the dark I fear trampling,
an effortless extinction of the spirit
underground: mass transit overflowing
onto dangerous edges of piers. It
connects palpably to suffocation,
a child's version of rape, vapid plots
of war movies—but who's the victim?
I used to envy the unrapable, not
for any power-mad apparatus curled
benignly in the bathwater, but for his
fortunate position outside of harm.
Or so I thought. Until the old man's arm
caught between the doors of the F train, his
mouth so close to mine I smelled his world.

2. Fear of Shoplifting

I've two teenage daughters, a decent
view of Hudson in winter, no regrets.
I'm too proud to accept support, yet men
seem to fear me. My daughters steal rent
and forage for the icebox with the G
missing from the GE and no egg slots.
Once, I saw my right hand lift a ten-spot
from the drawer at work where they trust me.
I kept it several days to see how
it would feel, but it smoldered inside.
My daughters laugh as they empty pockets
of hairspray and double-A batteries, trinkets
no young American should live without—
whatever society provides.

3. Fear of Politics

Like Geraldine Ferraro, I grew
prettier with age, primarily
due to hindsight and profound relief
when the worst things I'd ever dreamed came true
one by one and I lived through them. She,
as token, accomplished little, but I
enjoyed her quips in the *New York Times*
and voted—my first concession since Jackie
split the eighth grade girls down the middle.
Boys called me names that year. I was fat,
four-eyed, and my cheekbones were too freckled
to impress the soon-to-be-hormoned half
of St. Anne's School. It's easier to get
pregnant than it is to get elected.

4. Fear of Ritual

Yesterday I watched a young boy steal
a bicycle on Horatio—first
the shattered metal, then the peddling fast
as if for life—and a woman, beaten
by her boyfriend on 10th Street. Power
seems to sift through my fingers like pennies.
I think I could despise society
for its aberrations, myself for
my complicity—how on and off,
like the persistent colors of March,
I fear the rituals: jazz and reggae
of the subway; East Village cafés
spilling, impatient, onto Spring sidewalks;
a soprano with no hands in Central Park.

My Daughter Calls from a Halfway House in Houston

It was the same day they
found the bones
of a child buried
beneath the Bronx school steps,
the day I walked
to the museum while
someone knifed the Smith boy
and someone else held
a baby as shield in a shootout.

I stood before the red hills
of O'Keeffe's New Mexico,
her velvet iris, the black
centers of orange poppies,
and cried.

I had no choice.
I was staring at the faces
of children and they
were so beautiful.

Photographing Horses

The horses are so lucid, they pose
for shots in Central Park, their stiff ears
sideways against the wild children, their
daydreams masterfully concealed. Don't
envy the gentry their aging splits
of Piper in dark cellars reserved for
convivial occasions, all this
trotting around Manhattan for pleasure
in the parched middle of the day. Even
horses should be sleeping in clover,
their shoes kicked off with nothing but flies
to distract them. Consider their blinders,
the cracks in their feet from serving greed, eyes
closed with soot, those relentless whims of children.

Stations

1. 103rd Street

Something long forgotten flits
across concrete and my mind
startles into focus: a child
spread-eagled on suburban sidewalk,
neck twisted in some peculiar way.

I'm eight or nine, the child my best
friend accustomed to violent falls.
I've seen her on the ground before,
slept beside her beneath down quilts
and held her hand, afraid she'd

swallow her tongue in the night. I've
shared dry clothes with her, whispered:
"No one saw you, I swear." This man
lives underground. I've seen him
sleeping on cold platforms, begging

dimes for wine. He says: "Hungry. Jobless."
Today, there's a blue comb jammed
between his teeth; he jerks softly as
I walk around him, dark pool spreading
beneath him as I board the train.

2. 125th Street

We arrive at Harlem's westside station,
and three small boys, climbing on seats, swinging
from poles, entertaining us with their
rainbow of dazzling legs and faces, stop
and stare from the sooty windows, mouths
gaping like the buildings below, dark
silence and devastation. And Edgar,
the oldest, with the Goofy nose and ears
on his hat like a crown of innocence, says:
"There's the houses the fascists tore down." It's
no rare morning on the Broadway local,
everyone stiff as usual, hiding, hung-
over from booze or crack or malnutrition,
eyes begging sleep, no one listening but me.

3. 137th Street

If you remain in the city, you'll
squeeze through turnstiles easily, ride
subways for nothing—small consolation
for your poverty and hacked-up pride.

I know this by observation, but also
by something like a tight screw inside me.
And I suspect the metaphors of white
well-meaning people like me who

say blackberry blackberry blackberry while
hate exists in the morning: the other side
of beauty, the slavery of two cultures—
one to powerlessness, one to greed. Light

begins in sun and travels through shadow
like the bright eye of a subway car as
a transit man sprinkles sand on last night's
vomit, thankful for the job, holding his breath.

The New Frontier

They're about to capture
Harlem, make it
safe for my white skin while
they push color northward,
gentrify the Black race slowly
to extinction.

I wonder where the ace
of trump hides himself, which
renovated tenement he
sleeps in with his
Aryan taste and Third Reich whimsy.

When '25th Street falls, I'll
self-destruct near the Apollo
Gift Shop, my bones scatter
to the four winds where
they'll collide with God
and bring his Black ass home.

Divestment

I stand amidst cheers of young
history-making America, vortex
of wealth and well-meaning
shouts of "Divest now!"—
foot-stomping threat to trustees as
a young woman, center-stage, says: "Look
at South Africa." She doesn't say:
"Look at me." She doesn't say: "My
brothers are dying of hopelessness,
killing each other for crack."
She doesn't say: "My mother
abuses eight children
on Jamaican rum, my mother
at the Post Office thirty years,
commemorative stamps around her
like insults." She doesn't say:
"You're destroying us here
in Harlem, in Riverdale. You're
stealing our homes, our self-
esteem, our future." She says:
Apartheid, Uzi, children dying
in Africa. I hear: America.

Horace Mann School
April 10, 1989

17

Africa

1.

She yells at them but they don't hear—those
winos wouldn't understand a word
from a mind clear as the Hudson river
much less that high-grade lake of hers. She snaps:
"What would your mamas say, grown men like you,
out on the streets smellin' like dead dogs
and got the nerve to flirt?" It's true, one of them
just touched the hem of her skirt and said
something, but who knows what, his tongue's
stuck to the roof of his mouth. Everyone's
laughing but her. Still, she loves them the way
she loves mornings. When there's smog all over
Manhattan, she feels the blue air beneath,
full of hope and clean, the way God made it.

2.

She walks slower than anyone else
in New York. Up the subway stairs, nice
and easy. Times Square: So slow she pisses off
the tourists from Staten Island. It's her
way of wrestling demons: Calm down, walk
slower than they do. She's got her knife
nestled in a hip pocket, her glasses
dark as the Brooklyn Battery; claims
she sees everything when she's walking

at thirty-three and a third speed. As if
her life were long-playing, as if she knew
how to stretch things out to mean something.
Once, high as the World Trade, she slipped between
subway cars. And lived to remember.

3.

Stepping into Sloan's Supermarket, she
looks like a hoodlum and they follow her
from lettuce to canned tuna with their eyes, not
trusting the honesty of her pockets
or her desire to pay for what she eats,
drinks, smokes, pours to scour her stained wood floor.
She ignores them the way she ignores
anyone in power with a weapon
or privileged flesh. Still, it hurts, this undue
attention to the clothes she wears against
her brothers' twisted sexuality.
Some say the city belongs to Satan,
and she looks him deep in the eye as
she crosses his palm with salvation.

4.

Her son is eleven and still drug-free, sleeps
with his Nintendo snug against the soles
of his feet, trusts no one, especially
the uncle who visits in the night, wired
on poverty, anesthetized to the hopes

of a young boy whose class calls him "Professor."
Too many people have vanished, loved ones
there for Saturday morning cartoons,
missing by "Saturday Night Live." Why
try? In school the teacher prods him to learn,
talks about 6th grade graduation as if
Michael Jackson will be there, as if
his father will suddenly look at his watch
and walk through the door as the march begins.

5.

Her own father's invisible. She
called him once in '83 to see
if he still lived, but he wasn't home
so she buried him in her mind. Name's
Angelo. Sometimes she thinks she sees him
on the street and her heart flips before it
jumps to her mouth. What the hell would she say,
Hey, I'm your daughter, remember me? She's
sculpting a woman with a dull chisel.
The woman's pregnant, big ass, round breasts,
nothing like her bony frame, but her son
still grew inside her, came out head first,
ripe, and screaming. Was it wrong to want him?
Would that hole inside her belly ever heal?

6.

She makes an altar for her child self:
rose petals, candles, incense surrounding
old photographs and new ones of her son,
her lover, her, genuinely smiling.
No one's ever seen this side of her. Even
she wonders who is this woman now
that struggle seems redundant, studs and leather
gather dust on the closet door. Where
is the crippled child? They used to call her
stupid, beat her between the legs with knotted
rope, fuck her until she fled her body.
Special things she places on her altar:
A lime-green lollipop, a ruby ring,
a handful of earth from Africa.

Blood

I believe in the power of blood. Once,
Lori looked at a dying man
on the 1 train. He was
bleeding from the mouth while commuters
filed past the guarded car and gawked
through the window at his
ruined face, the brand name
of his only sneaker. "He could
be black or white," she told me,
"old or young. Come on—look!" But I know
how fear throws its image on my mind,
how it lies awake nights, breathing
demons in my ear: a child
murdered in Little Rock, 1959,
the screeching car, the thud
of flesh on dry earth. Lori
looked twice at the dying man,
and fear, lurking on the platform,
scurrying from the third rail, seized
her brain and sank its fingers deep until
she shoved her way onto the next train home,
dreamed of striking a small, blonde
woman, although she'd never
struck a woman before.

Waiting for the Bus in Kingsbridge

We discovered the sleeping pigeons while
huddled in a doorway of the Bank of New
York one cold night when we happened to look up.
There, on a beam beneath the el, ten,
fifteen, quiet birds, heads tucked into chests,
several lying down, several preening;
and we felt as if we'd come upon sacred
ground in the middle of the Bronx, as if
we stood in the presence of innocents.
And we thought of all the birds of the city
asleep on high wires, window ledges, hidden
by darkness or neon, or simply
unnoticed by humans below, how
until that night we'd called them rats with wings.

Rapper

for C.

The morning he pressed his suicide clothes
and dropped his ID in plastic so
they'd know who he was when he drowned, the tide
refused to take him out to sea. Behind
headphones of rap and frames with dark lenses,
he'd curled in on himself, a wave destined
to redance patterns as if his life
were this patch of sand in Rockaway. Why
remember his children now, that taste
of bile and salt that already crazed
his mind and shattered his final nerve—his past,
their future inside him like the fast
words in his ears—hymns of grief and plunder,
the rage of generations turned outward.

Citicard

1.

The city harbors loved ones:
Lori in Harlem where
people are the only glue
holding buildings up; Jenn
crosstown in rehab, Gracie
Mansion out her window
like a doll house with a small
mayor. Years back, I felt warmth
from your sidewalks, NY.
Before crack and condoms, Jennie
dropping acid into wine coolers.
Before I slept guiltlessly
with a woman. I'm part
of your decadence, Manhattan, rock
island of my grandfather's birth,
port of immigrant and art.
I mourn your passing into filth
and spit beneath my feet,
the stealing of your gentry
into Harlem, that straining
for a slice of sky.

2.

He slaps me with his headlights,
wraps his power trip around me
of steel and chrome, new
paint peeling onto asphalt. "Hey,"
he yells, "Prepare to die." Once
I had flesh the city could
pierce with a frown—
I'd bleed into sewers like rain.
Men without legs on subways
moved me, women with swollen
feet. Now I belong to them.
When I ignore them,
it's with the confusion
of the newly damned—
as if I believe I've survived.

3.

I want a Citicard of my own.
I want the luxury of free
checking, the rush
of large withdrawals. To take
that little card when
it's raining and the subway
smells like piss and pain
and stick it deep
in the heart of the city.

The Green Girl

"If one probes the metaphors of the forest, one senses
that the city is just another part of the forest anyway."
                                    —Jo Going

Last night I danced beside Melissa.
Each time she touched me—shoulder, knee, back
of hand—I leapt, like John in Elizabeth
at the sight of Mary pregnant with death
and resurrection. We danced at the Saint—
human planetarium, East Village dome

of stars not unlike the heavens of Maine—
until two: Two unsainted women watching
business suits hit on tank tops and high
heels of every sect and denomination.
Close by, the torrid investigation
of "zoning calisthenics" continued

in Manhattan—the "rampaging gigant-
ism," as Huxtable called it in the *Times*,
all the "striped and spired buildings" looming
long and shadowed across Central Park where
the young employeds move in with no apparent
ill will toward the homeless. Melissa

constructs a red chair in the Maine woods
and raises it with straps and pulleys
to the top of an elm. Her head butts the clouds
like a spire, her legs dangle. Below,

27

hands over their eyes in question marks,
friends try to talk her down, not laughing or
leaping in recognition of the divine
humor. Now there's ambivalence as
I attempt art in this leafless room.
Three times robbed—triple locks and killer cats
somehow circumnavigated—I float
three regulation basketballs in

a large polluted aquarium, rescue
globes from a trash bin and paint them black
and black, simulating reality.
I purchase five digital alarm clocks
from a sidewalk sale, several gold and red
lava lamps, a dozen enamel pots

and display them aesthetically while
Melissa sings a song of redwings
and thin air in the forest of Maine. Soon
she will lift off, leave her body in blue
shirt behind her like a mirage; and
the digital clocks of New York will click

at dawn, everyone sleep through the alarm.

Mantras of the Homeless

"I got a job, man. My job is askin' you for a quarter."
—Anonymous, the Bronx

He wears an Emily Dickinson t-shirt,
royal blue to match
his Yankees baseball cap. Smells
neglected. Everyone
cramped in small-ass subway seats
ignores him as he
reveals his secrets: AIDS,
Agent Orange. No one
believes him or offers change. A clown
came through the other day
and frightened children.
Once a man instructed us
on homosexuality, Jesus
coming on a cloud. We saw
a woman from the neighborhood
limp by on swollen feet,
period stains on her jeans. She was
too thin to look at. She said:
"God bless you" and "Have a nice day"
as if she meant it.

Witness

after the sculpture of Aristide Maillol — MOMA, Manhattan

The woman caught in the subway door
flies like a deer down the platform, feet
barely brushing concrete. Soon, I fear,
she'll smash against the graffiti'd wall—
a martyr to rapid transit—but
she breaks away and tumbles safely
toward the astonished mass of bystanders
holding its breath near the turnstiles. If

this vision seems mythical now as
a goddess cast in lead falls agelessly
into the cool museum fountain, it's
not that the woman—young, my height, white
dress, heels—fails to die. It's that my mouth,
filled with dying women, fails to stop the train.

Inheritrix

This past weekend of teenagers—I've got two
at opposite ends of hell—Autumn
finally chilled us all into wool
and tams and hands linked through arms, sunk deep
into warm pockets. And a young girl,
who'd been stabbing Upper West Side women
with hat pins or AIDS-infected needles
(no one knew for sure), turned herself in, while
parents loved her through their confusion. She was
filled with the spirit of "Thunderbird," chastened
by the fear of the "Lord Crack." She is
our promise, our new blood. Anyone
who ignores her prolongs the sin. Listen
to her cry the size of a pinprick.

How to Pray with
a Dying Woman

Robin's Egg Blue

I'm told they're mating now,
full of magical noise
that draws the day closed. I wish

I knew the name
of the fat robin who
builds her nest in the eaves,

so low I can almost touch her.
Last night, my body
flew to the ceiling as

he dreamed his way
inside me, reeking
of scotch. No. It was

day-old wine and garlic. I know
this is not possible. I was
out of my body. It was

my heart that flew away and
my body that lay in bed breathing
shallow breaths. As a child,

I was handled violently
by someone who believed violence
good for the soul.

This cannot be proven. I know
this is not believable. But
when he forced himself

through that gentle opening
I had no choice. I said
yes and abandoned my body,

my robin's egg blue
body, not knowing any other
way to the light.

Hysteria

The woman is dying
of childbirth. The room
is sterile with high
windows, and the rain
moves solemnly over glass.

She's dying in the rain
as she predicted.
I've seen this film
a dozen times and I know
her powerlessness.

In the nursing home,
my grandmother bites my mother
on the cheek—
a strong teething infant.
I predict another decade

of broken flesh, crushed glass
in bare hands. This
for the years someone
stole from her lap
like skeins of yarn.

Today, the Supreme
Court ruled any state
has power to restrict abortion.
Women will die now,
but it will be their own fault.

Two important things
have happened in my life:
One, my husband left me, and two,
with small children. Now
I no longer fear death.

I predict I'll die old
and ready, loosing my grip
like a film star on Hollywood—
near the Hudson, naked
behind the wheel of a VW Bug.

Healing

for Lisbeth

Burn a tick with the hot tip
of a match or flick it
into the owl's mouth that yawns

in the pine tree. Your old dog
is sick with cancer. Does it matter less
that she dies of something unseen,

that a woman caught in the rage
of men is new to Manhattan
and no one knows her name?

The owl asks questions
of the tree. The bumblebee
buzzes in the primrose.

You came to the sea for light. Why
feel sorrow as Mercedes limps
happily after seagulls?

This summer, men can't describe
their hatred of women.
They move among us

like knives, vicious
as unloved children, surrounded
by steel that blocks out sun.

Mercedes rests beside you as you work,
sated ticks dotting her coat
like random bullets.

When you remove them, one by one,
she lies quiet, trustful,
as if nothing you do could hurt her.

Provincetown
June, 1989

40

Reading Irving on the Steps of Juilliard

I wonder if he idolizes women
or wishes we were dead. I take everything
personally, my kids say, so it must
be true, this inability to deflect
every sun's rays on my flesh. Today,
a good friend told me she has cancer—deep
as a vein of gold in her right breast.
I'm not sure what her life has to do
with one writer's ambivalence toward women.
Or the respected school of dance where
nipples have been taped and non-threatening
for years. Or the homeless woman who
lounges on the bench like a goddess, her
breasts relaxing in her ocean blue coat.

Her Story of the World

The years with a man I tried
to sleep with one eye open
for the stranger in the morning.
It was useless. No glue
or toothpick proved successful
against the propagation
of the race.

We went down to the ocean,
but his power was oblique, his
wisdom finite, and I
was looking for that salt
beneath my fingernails.

Imagine kissing a woman
and not finding it disgusting!
Once I swallowed an oyster live.

I'll not be noticed
in the history of the world. Yet
neither will anyone write of me:
"She had no enemy," for he
will leave our children something
better than love, he says—
he feels this passionately
as he feels the fear
of dying without pockets.

But the ocean is powerful, wise.
Everyone knows this, it's no secret.
A woman can be near it
and need nothing.

As a child I learned to cry,
to trust in vulnerability,
and it has never let me down.

The Runner

She must leave New York,
but every woman she
knows in Santa Fe's
been raped. Even

in Provincetown,
a man held her wrist
until her frantic Shepherd
made him bleed. He was
a surfer from the sea she trusted.

Her sister in Illinois
earns karate belts,
her lover carries a knife
in Yellowstone Park.

She herself is ready
at a moment's notice to
swallow the capsule
she holds beneath her tongue
like a secret. Men

call her dangerous.

Mystic

She's on her back to a long-haired man who
cuts circles in pantyhose for his
private parts, that dangle, threateningly,
above her like dead leaves. Her husband
pours liquor in the kitchen for her sore
vertebrae, watches the progress of his
boyhood friend's penis in net stockings,
wondering if the woman's power
can reverse hopelessness. The debate
concerning morality has passed. He loves
the woman's longing, would happily share it
with any friend. Once he imagined her
beneath his Doberman, the dog moaning,
the woman comatose with abandon.
Yesterday, he hugged her as she lay
on his belly, crying. Put his arms
around her and squeezed until she saw light.

Respectfully,
open her third eye,
sending violet,
indigo, moon light.
Tell her
there are hundreds
of people in the room,
more than she imagines:
they spill
into sky.
Ask her
to bless you.
Hold her
until she sleeps
and your hands
grow warm with life.

Alchemy of the Body

The 8:48

arrived late beneath the Tappan Zee
across from verdant Jersey, that swamp
of unoriginal sin. Seatons,
my father claims and documents in
courthouses and cemeteries throughout
the Garden State, fought in the Civil,
the Revolutionary; died famous
in the wars they waged: fireman, butcher, slave
owner from Carolina—and *there's*
the blood my family calls patrician. There's
the ineluctable Black, I've known it—
hammer in my belly like a hymn of fear—
that ageless rape of a woman, her rage
so deep it ignites the fire in me.

Pleiades

for Zoe

The enigmatic hill our parents
shoveled on their lawn
in place of the ailing elm seems
self-conscious, a pimple on the chin,
but we sit there anyway
like the other Seaton sisters who
guarded their family homestead
from urbanization. Oh, love

can do anything. You say
the last time you saw the Pleiades
this bright, you swallowed
a whole bottle of pills in gin,
hoping they might work.

If we lived closer,
would we take each other
for granted?
The morning you were born,
I was thirteen and tired
of crushes on boys. I thought
I'd loved you magically into existence.
That Monday, I went to school where
I'd soon get ulcers from not fitting
in, where the nuns courted me,
and I held your name in my mouth all day
like a poem.

Summer nights, Trout Valley seems
silent as the heavens.
Occasionally, someone drives by,
but our shadows above the hill
are not distracting. Our secrets
are small as stars.

Mercedes Contemplates a Dive
off Macmillan Wharf

for Lisbeth

The least light makes us point:
wings of a gull, dying star,
airplanes leaving Boston. The wind
above Macmillan whips our faces until
we see everything through saltwater, now
gold beams approaching the Cape,
the same we've seen in Truro with that
unearthly hovering. You say
no one's been abducted by aliens unless
she's encountered them first
in childhood. Wild with canine joy, your
pup, Mercedes, contemplates a dive, fifty
feet to the bay below where
seagulls bob and tease, and I
hide quietly in your shadow because
I can't remember, Lisbeth, I just
can't remember.

Glory Days

They hovered over me—
two housewives and a cloistered
nun. I felt five
hands on my shoulders,
one on my head while
they babbled in tongues, hoping
for an end to winter. I said:
Can you help me want my husband?
God can, they said. So—
Quiet in my chair, I felt
a stone loosen, their
voices mounting in nonsense—
as if God cared about desire!
And I had this clear
picture of a kitchen when
I was four, and my father
at the table, and my
mother going out the door,
and I started to cry.
Curious, I thought, while
the women prayed. Then
we all stopped as if
on cue, and the cloistered nun
said: You're healed.

That was years before
church and state seemed to fuse
in this country and Christ
became the dubious savior
of wealthy oversexed men.

I was young—I believed
in whatever helped me—
but before I began to melt, my
husband felt the prick of Satan
and succumbed to lust, worthy
predecessor of politicians
everywhere. I went on
to revel in the fruits
of his abandonment, and that April,
when the daffodils peaked,
I whispered: Hallelujah.

Triptych

1. Alchemy of the Body

after Ainslee Beery

The window in this room is pointless.
It opens on an airshaft that has
no air, no natural light, and every
paper airplane thrown in its current
drifts downward. Once I almost died here,
my veins fat with East Village ecstacy,
cobalt-blue, drug-induced light. Coming
back to my body was a tedious
and tender reality, a concrescence
of spirit, mind, flesh that devoured years.
Now this bust of sand and gravel sways
from the ceiling, and I stand naked
in a box of opalescence: transformed,
the light of my new skin performing.

2. Studies of Light

She will be naked.
She will paint herself the color
of oceans
and stand in a scrapwood
construction with a small door
and the invitation in a child's hand:
Open.

Think of the body:
Its resonance. Light
plays on the body
as if it were a lute
or a fiddle.

An ocean.

       * * *

In the box you'll see unexplained
phosphorescence, clearly
identifiable breasts, belly,
arms. When you

white light

touch her, you'll
scream softly, not having known
she was real.

       * * *

Ainslee speaks of light and the body:
"Is it possible not to want to paint them?"

And the woman in the box
will ripple imperceptibly.

An ocean.

3. Ainslee, Employed

She loses her body on a corner
in Soho—black shorts, shoes, white socks, white
t-shirt—far from Minnesota vending iced
cappuccino to sultry New Yorkers.
She conjures Minneapolis: a bridge
between cities, the Mississippi,
opaque and placid as thick coffee
she hands over, terrified. She wonders which
angel will save her, whose casual lips
welcome and soothe, whose sudden presence offer
passage. She sees herself in the distance,
bending, a slender choreographer,
trembling over urns and steamy secrets
she bestows upon the world like a dance.

The Giving

It's crucial I celebrate my friend's new film
in which my old Honda dies, demolished
in a grassy ditch in Croton-on-
Hudson to advance the plot and remove
the rusty sedan from my tangled hair.
It lodged there at a hundred thousand miles,
pistons still ticking, gas pumping, while I
stalled, unable to part with him her it,
the closest thing to God I've ever known, with
those cold morning starts, those unconditional
free miles. The filmmaker's name is Stockwell.
She says she was lucky to have that old
five-speed perform so graciously. In the film,
a mother of two barely survives the crash.

A mother of two barely survives the crash,
metaphorically depicting my thirties
when I offered myself to an odd
assortment of fellows who followed
in my former husband's footsteps. This is not
a story for children. When mine read it
I will deny authorship as easily
as I delivered them both, on a Sunday
morning, five years and three months apart. They
will grin with red faces and forgive me,
and I will vow not to involve them again
in my real life no matter how needed
their forgiveness. At the end of the film,
the children fall asleep in each other's arms.

The children fall asleep in each other's arms,
waiting for word of their mother. Mine
would stand at the door and wave, nights, when
I needed the company of men
to coax me from the somnambulism
of single parenthhood. Some would try to love
my daughters. Most would berate me while
fumbling with my newly-freed body, saying
my kids were walking all over me,
needed a man's hand to shape their lives. No
thank you. If spoiling them meant refusing
to use my clout as a grown-up or mold them
with fear and grandiosity, then
they're spoiled, I'm glad, and I'd do it again.

They're spoiled, I'm glad, and I'd do it again,
although at times I blame myself for
their undisguised indifference toward people they
don't particularly like, the blasphemous
behavior of thinking for themselves when
it's taken me all these years to find
the answers and they won't believe me.
Filmmakers have a desperate job, like
mothers, who pull ten strings at the same time. Still,
it must be worth it: we all go on making
films and children, sonnets, and a sky
full of other quarrelsome creations from
the chaoses of our lives, which is why
it's crucial I celebrate my friend's new film.

Truce

"It is written that one must drink until the good
cannot be distinguished from the bad."
      —E.M. Broner, *A Weave of Women*

Having drunk every available wine
without truce for long anonymous years,
my testimony yields this equation,
also of Broner: "After much laughing
is hiccuping and depression." See
how plump grapes mature without me, seldom
beckon the way they used to with their
tiny teeth reflecting light. Sodden now
with the sun rain moon and stars of life, I
nevertheless deplore the strenuous
questioning a clear, unwatered mind brings me,
evenings, when I'm thirsty and alone, my
diving into chilled Perrier a poor
substitute for Absolut and lime.

Laugh. You promised ninety days. It's over
nine years and unnamed arthropods still
inhabit my bloodstream—occasional
as their olympics might be—and still
make me crazy and certain I'm sane.
You said it's "grace" to feel—the threat of loss,
the breadth of every shiny fear. Perhaps
the proverb is right, but continuing
in this body with that conviction baffled
the hell out of me. I drank until

the good could not be distinguished from
the bad, and beauty lay in the Bowery
of my mind, mingled with a longing
for truce between my death and my life.

for Bill W.

Wintersong

After the concert in the Cathedral...for Paul Winter

So soon after solstice
here's Christmas, Christchild,
Christians with that otherworldly
look. I need sex and whispers.
I need collusion with a human,
not God in a manger, with trumpets.
I can't bear the lady on stage whose
aura can be plainly seen,
happy and blue, whose vocal
chords are made holy
by the water she drinks deep
in the bowels of the divine.
How bad I must be to say hallelujahs
seem cliché here, how
sad to give up the joy
of pagan rites. I expect
I'm an aberration when
carols squall against my inner
ear and I clock their invasion
as if the sons and daughters
of Whoever-Made-This-Beauty
were not enough to light
the Cathedral, as if God
were not minstrel after all—O
Paul, give me your ancient songs
and let the carols wait.
It's the old simplicity I seek:
Darkness, forgiveness, the fire
that invites back the sun.

"Music—Pink and Blue, II"

She swore until she died she
was not a woman's artist, not
concerned with women any more than, say,
bones.

Georgia, Georgia,
that's good enough for me.

The Sighting

Two people are murdered in Woodstock,
Illinois, a murder of gin and vengeance.
Their child—altar boy, A-student, murderer—
escapes to the Wisconsin Dells where
he's sighted on the water slide, now
entering the Cave of Mounds, now running
through the labyrinthine House on the Rock.
Back home, the neighborhood is bereaved,
bewildered.
      My sister, two blocks away
with her new baby, says: How do you stab
two people at the same time? And calls a friend
from bible study whose husband serves
as detective in Woodstock. What constitutes
a sighting? she asks. The woman is helpful,
confident. Her voice, evangelical,
helps Melissa through the night without
Dan who's delivering speedboats in Jersey.
I choose this day to tell her I'm gay.

The Bed

Christmas in the Midwest

I brought a lover home
in Midwest snow.
My parents said:
You sleep here, he there,
so we made love here
and there when the garage door slammed
and the house beat like a clock
around us. I dreamed

I was arrested
in a VW bug with the stickshift
hard against my leg
by the Cary police force shining
high beams on my breasts. Why
does sex ignite authority?

My parents received word
of my defection to women
peaceably. They pretended not
to be surprised—
"the way the world is…
the way men are…"—
and said they'd treat her
kindly at Christmas
as they would any female friend.

They made no mention
of "here and there." We slept
like children in a double bed
beneath handmade quilts,

tried heroically to stay afloat
without their disapproval, the headlights
of a straight society to validate us.

Grief

After the Ghanaian dancing, we fought
about monogamy, whether
to separate with it or without. Never
mind the impossibility
of sleeping near someone else's skin,
you said, you'd throw up! Well,
I could have watched them dance all
night, how could you
have fallen asleep? Once you snored,
and when I nudged you said: "I'm woke!"
Sure. Everyone around us clapping,
jerking in their seats, you
leaving for donuts during Sohu.
I loved the way their bright
asses monopolized the stage, those
drums like a thousand hungers. Maybe
you've heard them all your life,
maybe it's cliché to love the music
of your homeland. But no one else slept
at the finale, and when the medicine
woman, with the pot of herbs on her head
like the burden of a people, threw
holy water at the two of us,
maybe you didn't need the bath, but
I did. And I wonder: What does Africa
mean to a Black New Yorker? And why
did you hurt so hard you had to sleep?

Harlem

There was little more that summer
than gray pigeons in light-flecked
ginkgos, but there was
that, and we remarked on the light—
how the pigeons shook it loose
and trailed it down Lenox—
as if the sun had finally risen

over Harlem. And the hymns
those Sunday mornings like sighs
to Jesus or the naked
wishes of earth—naked
hands on backyard porches
clapping up storms, thunder
familiar as birthpain.

And the gospels inside
of sex and breakfast, soft
dishwater in the sink, how
we broke the glass of old
reflections and sprinkled ourselves
with the joy of salvation.
Little more that summer than

two women moving in love
near the fragile bones of old men
stacked in bombed-out doorways—
sweet God in heaven—

it was all we could do
to keep ourselves from burning up,
so hot the sun in our hearts.

Junebug

If Junebug were alive today, I'd kill him
for his wine-soaked excursions to your bed,
his drugged fumbling with your pajamas while
you protested in vain and your mother
held her breath in the next room. You told her
a dozen times how he wandered through
your nightmares, a demented father figure,
ignoring you profoundly by day, sucking
the life from your childhood at night. She
thought it was good for you, this schooling
with a hard-driven man, the kind who made
women out of mixed-up girls, straight arrows
out of baby dykes. But he's been dead for years,
and your mother's slowly dying of rum.

Snow

White people leave the express
at 96th Street, collectively,
like pigeons from a live wire
or hope from the hearts of Harlem.
And I'm one of them, although
my lover sleeps two stops north between
Malcolm X and Adam Clayton Powell
Boulevards, wishing my ass
were cupped inside her knees and belly,
wishing this in a dream thick
with inequalities.

I live on Riverside Drive. My face
helped get me here. I was
ruddy with anticipation the day
I interviewed for the rooms
near the park with its
snow-covered maples. I was full
of undisguised hope as I
strolled along the river, believing
I belonged here, that my people
inherited this wonderland
unequivocally, as if they deserved it.

My lover buys twinkies from the Arabs,
bootleg tapes on '25th,
and carries a blade in her back
pocket although her hands
are the gentlest I've known.
She ignores the piss smells

If you'd been male, I'd have despised your guts,
and we'd be slightly less visible—
therefore, safer in Manhattan. But
who knows? It seems Black and white couples
attract attention everywhere—at least
when they step gingerly out of shadows.
Once, we were waiting on 119th
for a gypsy cab and crazy Cornelius
Crowley came tottering off the curb
with pointed finger to lecture you
on the sins of sleeping with a white woman.
You became famous that night in Harlem
for your fleetness of foot and biting words,
the blade that emerged like a friend beside you.

The blade that emerged like a friend beside you
lay buried beneath our clothes the day
we first made love. The sky was rare blue,
the air bright as country air. I gave
you violets and tiger lilies, jewelry
of amethyst and moonstone, cowrie shell
and abalone pearl. You gave me
lapis and sunflowers, tiny bells
of polished gold. Our bed was sanctuary
from the ridicule around us, the hate
as daily as sunrise. We opened
to the lawlessness and luxuries
of love, the delightful possibilities and
a robin appeared in Harlem the same day.

The Painter

Light from your body swirls
on the south wall above
the dark blue comforter.
Literally: Light,
curled around your skin
like a sunrise. I've never
seen an aura before,
and I watch it
move as you move, up
and down to the rhythm
of your sleep. I know
your heat, how you
kick off covers at three A.M.
like a child in fever.
How your hair clings, damp
in the morning, my own hair
damp from your spilled dreams.

I was surprised
the first time you rose
over me with your black
eyes containing rainbows.
I'd pictured
a postcard life with white
picket fence, wed
upwardly mobile men and bore
their meaninglessness for years.
That woman went down
in Hudson salt where
Jersey meets York

with her gin and Catholicism, hit
bottom near the GW Bridge,
and found you
in Harlem, dreams splashed
on walls: crimson, coral, gold.

After the Bomb Threat at the Cathedral

In the blue
of December, the Russian
building rises, tallest
beacon in the West Bronx. Lori
upends the table we brought
from Harlem, glues it solid,
immovable as prejudice. We
sit at its unshaking
surface, watch
the Russians lean
into sunlight. Once,

six women
and a flatbed truck
carried me to a basement
with no heat. I was
running from men who
gossiped as if
injured, as if I spit them
into last night's garbage. I
moved from warm turret
to cellar glazed with ice, hid
for forty days and forty
more days until
I understood the sway
and degeneracy of love. Now

someone's selling
pieces of Berlin wall
for Christmas—
in festive boxes like pet
rocks, in resin
like paperweights while
Lori talks of flying dreams, how
a chair takes her high
above the Russian building,
how she knows she's gone
too far when
the air feels dangerous
as sex. Yesterday,

the Bishop ordained
his first gay minister. Today,
we stood in sub-zero
wind on Amsterdam, our breath
trumpets between us. Who
would harm us, we thought, two
fools holding hands
in the dark.

Scream

Why did you scream in the night as if
orgasms hurt, as if no one's blood
on that street boiled at your freedom? This
is what I remember: Machine gun shots
punctuating candlelit dinners. Men
commandeering homeless mutts as fodder
for their unmuzzled pit bull puppies. Once,
someone threw chunks of concrete at our door.
When a drunk attacked us at the corner, cops
urged us to press charges, but we refused,
saying: "We have to live here." I forget
how we moved through the daily jeers and threats.
Your reaction always astonished
and disappointed you: You were afraid.

White Balloon

"To love something you know will die is holy."
        —*Kaddish*, AIDS Memorial, New York, 1987

The air is gravid with life,
the cloudless sky swells
with souls, ascending.

I'm in charge of one young soul
tied to my wrist
with a string that won't break.

St. Veronica's, the end of June:
You weep beside me, hold
a candle steadily near the flame.

Earlier we were two ladies
shopping on Broadway. I recall
your wire of a body,

the delicate arc of ribs
and small breasts above—this
as you quick-changed

in search of something radical,
feminine. Your terror of pink
amused me. You said:

Don't tell anyone
of this sudden reversal. I said:
I will, but I'll change your name.

Linda, it's the letting go
that terrifies: the night air
alive with rising ghosts,

the cries of strong men
grieving in each other's arms,
the ease with which we love.

Poem Containing a Matrix Sentence

"After my mother beat my ass, I'd sleep
like a baby for days," she says, round
in my arms like this smooth egg nestled
in its envelope of wood. She sculpts
ceaselessly through white heat of August while
insects welt her incandescent skin, through nights
of raccoon and gold moon above the woodpile.
The woman I love is obsessed
with perfection, beginnings of life held
in suspended animation—like a babe
before disintegration of the matrix
and childlike hope begins. "The woman
is obsessed" is the matrix sentence, "I
love" the core of perfect life within.

Preposition

I console myself with
this pen found along
the Hudson where the universe dropped it after
I skimmed my wish over
the blackened water between
the Tappan Zee and the GM plant. I'd love to sleep near
you, if the tumbled days stopped for
a brief rest and all that static among
desires eased up;
if your present lover gave permission in
lyric form and our integrities bent beneath
imperfect visions we strapped ourselves into
and rode like a roller coaster down
where lust is a possible preposition to
love, at
least something clean worth taking note of,
a tide we innocently glide in on.

Beneath Skylight

Beneath skylight
and evening star
Venus
place of my birth
I speak to the woman
call her lover
She calls me
lover

I am aberrant
deformed
in childhood
or mind
somewhere
they say
I follow a lie

Why
woman
for a mate why
her softest of bodies
Any
man who
loves a woman
will understand

I would kill
for her

I bleed have
given birth
once screaming once
consoling
the child within
She
is the mother
of a son
who demands hugs

She gave me
this fever
I saw it
coming through her eyes

Any woman
who loves a woman
will understand

Spuyten Duyvil

It took weeks for my wrist to heal after your dream
invaded our sunrise and pinned my arm
to the king-sized bed. I said:
"It's me" but my white skin
blinded you or perhaps I was invisible,
as your family insists, and my wrist
was nothing in your hand but air, nothing
of bone that could fracture. My voice
dimmed beside the others
that obliterated wall, bed, sun on familiar sheets—
the same voices that begin: Hate
and end with the color of my skin.

Wake up: You're sleeping with a woman
whose fathers chained yours together, who
forced your grandmother to bear yellow children.
How will we heal?

I drive you to work, to the tip of the Bronx where
Harlem meets Hudson in a confluence
of bridges, and good and evil, and Dutch landlords
waiting to pay you peanuts for a day's labor.
Will it always be like this? My wrist
aching with grief at the wheel?

Spuyten Duyvil: (Dutch) To spite the devil.

The Bed

We build a bed
of plywood and carriage bolts,
hoist ourselves
high above earth, laughing
at the clarity of our dreams.

"Stop at any playground,"
they say, "single out
one little girl at hopscotch
or running down a slide, and think:
you were that young once,
that vulnerable."

We admire our bed,
its four corners fit together
in peace, the strength
of its wide platform. We inhale
the perfume of fresh-cut wood, dive
naked into grandma's quilt.

"Forgive yourself
your lack of vigilance in the night,
flesh that violated yours.
See how small you were,
how your white socks
dribbled into red shoes."

Nothing breaks when we love.
We fling ourselves
into mornings as if crazed,
confront the tired faces of night.
In our new bed,
we are miraculous.

About the Author

MAUREEN SEATON was born in Elizabeth, New Jersey, and raised in both rural and urban New York State. She has been a single mother of two daughters for over a decade while engaged in various jobs such as: teacher of high school English and English as a Second Language, electronics salesperson, secretary, and Therapeutic Touch Practitioner. She currently lives with her spouse, the sculptor, Lori Anderson, in New York City.*Fear of Subways* is Maureen Seaton's second book of poetry. Her first book, *The Sea Among the Cupboards*, won the Capricorn Award in 1990 and will be published by New Rivers Press in the fall of 1991.

ABOUT THE COVER ARTIST

LOUISE WILLIAMS is known for her intense images of women, birth and mothering. Her paintings express outrage at rape and murder on a global and a human scale and celebrate joy and the many facets of cerebral, sensual and spiritual love. Her work has been featured nationally, in one-person and group exhibitions; her most recent solo show was at Seattle Pacific University in 1990. Her work is included in the collections of the Apache Corporation, Ucross Foundation, Ellensburg Arts Commission and Evergreen State College among others. She has taught at many colleges and universities and is currently a full-time artist in Seattle. Louise Williams met Maureen Seaton at the Ucross foundation in 1987 when both were in residence. The affinity between them has continued from opposite coasts.

About the Book

MARCIA BARRENTINE designed the cover for *Fear of Subways*. She is a graphic designer and artist who lives in Portland, Oregon. The text typography was composed in Palatino. The cover typography was composed in Goudy Old Style. The book was printed on acid-free paper. *Fear of Subways* has been issued in a first edition of two thousand copies of which two hundred fifty are clothbound.

WINNERS OF THE
EIGHTH MOUNTAIN POETRY PRIZE

1989
THE EATING HILL
Karen Mitchell
Selected by Audre Lorde

1990
FEAR OF SUBWAYS
Maureen Seaton
Selected by Marilyn Hacker

OTHER BOOKS FROM
THE EIGHTH MOUNTAIN PRESS

TRYING TO BE AN HONEST WOMAN
Judith Barrington
1985

COWS AND HORSES
Barbara Wilson
1988

HISTORY AND GEOGRAPHY
Judith Barrington
1989

A FEW WORDS IN THE MOTHER TONGUE
POEMS SELECTED AND NEW (1971–1990)
Irena Klepfisz
Introduction by Adrienne Rich
1990

DREAMS OF AN INSOMNIAC
JEWISH FEMINIST ESSAYS, SPEECHES AND DIATRIBES
Irena Klepfisz
Introduction by Evelyn Torton Beck
1990

INCIDENTS INVOLVING MIRTH
Anna Livia
1990

MINIMAX
Anna Livia
1991

AN INTIMATE WILDERNESS
LESBIAN WRITERS ON SEXUALITY
Judith Barrington, Editor
1991